EYE TO EYE WITH DOGS

BEAGLES

Lynn M. Stone

Rourke
Publishing LLC
Vero Beach, Florida 32964

www.rourkepublishing.com

PHOTO CREDITS: All photos © Lynn M. Stone

Cover: *Beagle-type dogs have been around for more than 2,000 years. Their ancestors probably came from Italy, France, and England.*

Acknowledgments: For their help in the preparation of this book, the author thanks humans June Connelly, Jeannine Price of Blackhawk Beagles (Mount Morris, IL) and Catherine Cushing; and canines Lucy, Doughty's Digger, Annie, Tinkerbelle, and others.

Editor: Frank Sloan

Cover and page design by Nicola Stratford

Library of Congress Cataloging-in-Publication Data

Stone, Lynn M.
     Beagles / Lynn M. Stone.
         p. cm. — (Eye to eye with dogs)
     Summary: A brief introduction to the physical characteristics, temperament, uses, and breeding history of the beagle.
     Includes bibliographical references (p.).
     ISBN 1-58952-325-3
     1. Beagle (Dog breed)—Juvenile literature. [1. Beagle (Dog breed). 2. Dogs.] I. Title.

SF429.B3 S76 2002
636.753'7—dc21   2002017840

Printed in the USA

MP/W

Table of Contents

The Beagle   5

Popular Dogs   8

Beagles of the Past   11

Looks   17

Beagle Companions   18

A Note About Dogs   22

Glossary   23

Index   24

Further Reading/Websites   24

Beagles are small, playful dogs that love to explore.

The Beagle

The beagle is a good-natured little dog with a big voice. "Beagle" may have come from an old French word that meant "open throat." It may also have come from an old English word that meant "small." In either case, the beagle seems to have been well named.

BEAGLE FACTS	
Weight:	18-30 pounds (8-14 kilograms)
Height:	12-15 inches (30-38 centimeters)
Country of Origin:	Great Britain
Life Span:	12-15 years

Beagles are one of the **breeds** in the hound group. The beagle looks like a miniature version of the foxhound and **harrier**.

A beagle is very like a foxhound, pictured here.

Hot on the trail, an airborne beagle clears a hurdle of corn stalks.

Beagles are often called **scenthounds** because of their keen sense of smell. Hunters train beagles to log onto rabbit scent. A trained beagle will **flush** rabbits for the hunter. As the rabbit runs, the hunter can shoot at it.

Popular Dogs

Most beagles are not trained hunters. Beagles are popular for other reasons. One of them is the beagle's loving personality. Another is that a beagle is about the size of a loaf of bread. Homes that can't hold a big hound can hold a beagle.

By the year 2001, the American Kennel Club (AKC) listed the beagle as the fifth most popular breed. The Canadian Kennel Club (CKC) listed the beagle as number eleven.

A beagle takes its master for a stroll.

Scenthounds like the beagle have a keen sense of smell.

Beagles of the Past

Hounds have been around for hundreds of years in different sizes and shapes. Hounds are dogs that were developed to chase and catch mammals. Some hunt mostly from sight, like greyhounds. Others, like the beagle and foxhound, hunt by scent.

The exact roots of the beagle are impossible to know. Beagle type dogs have been known for more than 2,000 years. It is likely that the modern beagle has **ancestors** from Italy, France, and certainly England. One of those ancestors may have been the harrier. Harriers date back at least 800 years in England.

With its short legs, a beagle is easier to follow than a long-legged hound.

The modern beagle (shown here) was developed from longer-legged British hounds.

Early dog **breeders** wanted a small hunting hound that they could follow on foot. They also wanted a hunting dog they could actually pick up and carry in a pocket. The result was the beagle.

Beagles of old came in many sizes. Some were just 9 inches (23 centimeters) tall. The modern beagle was developed in the mid-1800s in England.

The AKC recognizes two varieties of beagles. One variety has a maximum height of 13 inches (33 cm) at the shoulders. Beagles of the larger variety can be up to 15 inches (38.5 cm) tall.

Its small size makes a beagle easy to hug.

Basset or beagle? Long, drooping ears and low-slung belly identify this hound as a basset.

Looks

A beagle has large, round, floppy ears and a square **muzzle**. It has a short-haired coat. The coat is usually a mix of white, tan, and black. A beagle's tail is long and curves up slightly.

Beagles are sometimes confused with basset hounds. Bassets are about the same height. The stout, short-legged bassets, however, may weigh twice as much as a beagle!

Beagle Companions

Beagles love the companionship both of humans and other dogs. Left alone, a beagle may bark and howl.

Beagles love company—canine or human—and many owners keep several beagles in a pack.

A beagle's wet, black muzzle is the nose of a hunter.

Beagles arc at their best when they can divide time between the home and the outdoors. Indoors, beagles are calm but playful.

Outdoors, beagles love to explore. All dogs live in a world of smells. But the little beagle is more a slave to its snout than many breeds. Nose to the ground, a beagle will busily search for new scents. Sometimes the scent leads a beagle to run off. Even trained beagles can be stubborn when they're on the trail of a fresh scent.

Some beagle owners enter their dogs in field trials. Field trials test a dog's ability to follow commands for outdoor tasks.

A beagle and its trainer take a training time-out.

A Note About Dogs

Puppies are cute and cuddly, but buying one should never be done without serious thought. Choosing the right breed of dog requires some homework. And remember that a dog will require more than love and great patience. It will require food, exercise, grooming, a warm, safe place to live, and medical care.

A dog can be your best friend, but you need to be its best friend, too. For more information about buying and owning a dog, contact the American Kennel Club at: http://www.akc.org/index.cfm or the Canadian Kennel Club at http://www.ckc.ca/.

Glossary

ancestors (AN ses tuhrz) — those in the past from whom an animal has descended; direct relatives from the past

breeds (BREEDZ) — particular kinds of domestic animals within a larger group, such as the beagle breed within the dog group

breeders (BREE duhrz) — people who raise animals, such as dogs, and carefully choose the mothers and fathers for more dogs

flush (FLUSH) — to chase or frighten an animal out of its hiding place

harrier (HAH ree ur) — an old, long-legged breed of English hound

muzzle (MUZ uhl) — the nose and jaws of an animal; the snout

scenthounds (SENT hownz) — hounds that use their noses more than their eyes to follow an animal

Index

American Kennel Club
  8, 14

bassets 17

breeders 13

breeds 6

Canadian Kennel Club 8

field trials 20

foxhound 6, 11

harrier 6, 12

hounds 6, 8, 11

rabbits 7

scent 7, 11, 20

sense of smell 7

Further Reading

Vallila, Andrew. *Guide to Owning a Beagle*. Chelsea House, 1999
Wilcox, Charlotte. *The Beagle*. Capstone, 1998

Websites to Visit

http://www.k9web.com

About the Author

Lynn Stone is the author of over 400 children's books. He is a talented natural history photographer as well. Lynn, a former teacher, travels worldwide to photograph wildlife in its natural habitat.